The Temptress Academy, owned and operated by Cher Sarkisian and her longtime friend Christina Aguilera, has become the world's leading music company, engaged in recording, music publishing, merchandising, and audio-video content. The academy has an impeccable reputation as a fair and honest company, and it's renowned for its prestigious award, the Cleopatra.

n recent years, advances in artificial intelligence have exposed major companies like Universal, Warner, Spotify, and others as corrupt, plagued by sanctions, money laundering, bribery, discrimination, plagiarism, copyright infringement, and piracy. Artists, recording studios, publishing companies, and merchandising firms were leaving these corporations in droves, flocking to the Temptress Academy, which was celebrated for its integrity. The academy's stellar

The Temptress Academy

By

Keith Ragnvald

reputation made it a target, and the corrupt companies would stop at nothing to destroy it. Their attacks were relentless.

Cher was at her home office in Malibu, where floor-to-ceiling windows and glass patio doors opened out to the sandy beach and the vast Pacific Ocean beyond. She sat at a large antique Victorian mahogany desk, with a towering mahogany bookshelf behind her, displaying her many awards and honors. Sipping a glass of wine, Cher gazed at the ocean, only to be startled by a whirling sound. A drone appeared on the balcony, its tiny red and white LED lights blinking as if watching her—because it was. An oval-shaped camera lens was attached to the front of the drone, and after a few brief moments, seemingly verifying its location, a flap on the bottom of the drone dropped open. A small box, about ten inches square, fell onto the balcony. The flap snapped shut, and the drone spun around 180 degrees before whirring off into the distance, disappearing from sight.

Cher stared at the box for several minutes, debating whether to investigate. Her home was equipped with the latest technology, including advanced security tied into the Temptress Academy's quantum supercomputer. The deck's security cameras quickly scanned the box, running several tests in seconds. Satisfied that it posed no danger, Cher brought the box inside and placed it on her desk.

It was known as a "gypsy box," a type of package with no way to trace its sender or origin. Cher knew it would contain a glyph recording—a hologram designed to convey a message. The box had a flap on top with a twist-lock mechanism. When Cher turned the lock to the open position, the flap automatically began to lift. As it opened, it activated a camera inside the box that conducted a facial recognition scan, confirming that Cher was the intended recipient. Once verified, the box's top flap fully opened, and the four sides unfolded. A laser from the camera projected an image above the box—large block letters forming a message.

Cher's mouth dropped open in disbelief as she read the words: Christina had been kidnapped. The ransom? Surrender all copyrights, labels, merchandising, and audio/video content, or the Temptress Academy would be destroyed.

At the end of the message, a clip played, showing Christina blindfolded and being forced into an aircraft. The faces of her captors were blurred, making them unrecognizable. Cher's fury boiled over. This had gone too far. She would make them pay dearly. She knew she couldn't comply with their demands—doing so was not an option. Whoever had done this wasn't going to simply release Christina. They intended to kill her or worse.

Christina had been performing a residency show at the Venetian in Las Vegas for the past three months. Cher quickly called the studio, and her worst fears were confirmed: Christina had vanished without a trace.

Cher immediately sent out a message from her phone. She would need Andrea Stolpe and the songwriters' help—urgently. Andrea Stolpe and the songwriting team were a key branch of the Temptress

Academy, dedicated to protecting artists, publishers, playwrights, record labels, and studios from attacks—whether they were cyber threats, copyright infringement, plagiarism, bribery, or piracy. They also provided personal security. With the rise of artificial intelligence, deepfakes had become rampant in the industry, and the Temptress Academy remained hyper-vigilant against these attacks. Cher needed them now more than ever, to find out who was behind this and where Christina was being held.

Andrea was at the Temptress Academy office, enjoying her morning tea, when Cher's urgent message arrived. Without wasting a moment, Andrea sent a message to her assistant, Madison. When Madison entered the coffee room, Andrea quickly explained the situation. Andrea instructed her to send an urgent call to the team, and with a few taps on her iPad, Madison notified everyone to meet at the office.

Andrea and Madison made their way downstairs to the building's main lobby. As they crossed the lobby floor toward the elevator, Myles and Lumina walked in through the front entrance. They all joined Andrea and Madison in the elevator, and Madison pressed the button for the building's lowest floor.

As the elevator descended, Andrea filled Myles and Lumina in on the situation. They were headed to the floor where the Temptress Academy's quantum supercomputer was housed—one of the most powerful computers in the world. Capable of breaking the exascale speed barrier, it was liquid-cooled, equipped with over 5 terabytes of flash memory, and operated with 4 GPLs powered by 3rd generation

CPUs, totaling 9 million cores optimized for high-performance computing. This supercomputer had the unique ability to detect deepfakes and AI-driven fraud within the music industry.

Tom and Angela, the songwriters responsible for looking after Christina during her Las Vegas residency at the Venetian, were en route to the office. While they waited, Andrea entered all the available information into the system, including tracking Christina's phone and accessing the Venetian's security cameras. The data was immediately fed into the quantum supercomputer.

When Tom and Angela arrived, Tom explained that they had watched Christina's show the previous night and had escorted her back to her penthouse suite. Sometime after midnight, she had been taken. By 7 a.m., Christina's manager was unable to reach her, and her room was found empty.

Before long, the supercomputer started returning results. They discovered that Christina was trapped in a state of quantum probability—an effect created by a specialized quantum computer. This state was achieved by an energy pulse containing only half a unit of energy, causing the particle, or in this case, Christina, to exist in both the spin-up and spin-down states simultaneously, according to quantum laws. Very few computers in the world were capable of such a feat, and it was only a matter of time before they identified who was responsible.

Cher already had her suspicions. A few months ago, Merck Mercuriadis had approached her about buying out the Temptress Academy. When Cher refused, Merck had been visibly upset, muttering a threat about a hostile takeover through gritted teeth. Merck Mercuriadis was the CEO of Hipgnosis Song Fund, a British Guernsey-registered music IP investment and song management company. Listed on the London Stock Exchange and funded by the equity firm Blackstone, Hipgnosis had been losing shareholder value for years. After spending billions acquiring the music catalogs of artists like Christina McVie, Neil Young, Ed Sheeran, Red Hot Chili Peppers, Bon Jovi, Justin Bieber, and many more, the company was teetering on the edge of collapse. Accusations of fraud and misuse of funds were swirling, and it seemed Merck's desperation had driven him to dangerous extremes.

There had been other attempts to acquire the Temptress Academy, either through buyouts or mergers. Universal Music, a subsidiary of Vivendi, had made a recent offer just last week. CEO Leo Lucian Grainge approached Cher with a merger proposal, but she had politely declined. Apple Music, Spotify, and Pandora (Sirius XM) also had their eyes on the Academy's success, and many would stop at nothing to achieve what the Temptress Academy had built.

Cyber-attacks were a constant threat to the Academy, as were virtual attacks on their clients during performances, at recording studios, and even during rehearsals. Often, AI-generated deepfakes were used to mimic artists, attempting to steal their work. However, thanks to the combined efforts of Cher, Christina, Andrea, the songwriting team, and the Academy's quantum supercomputer, they had managed to thwart these attacks. But this kidnapping had taken things to a whole new level, showing just how far their adversaries were willing to go.

When Cher entered the boardroom of the Temptress Academy, Andrea Stolpe, along with Myles, Madison, Lumina, Tom, and the rest of the songwriting team, were already seated around the large table. Cher walked to the podium at the front of the room and activated the projector, which displayed the findings from their investigation. As they suspected, Hipgnosis was behind Christina's kidnapping. A picture of Merck Mercuriadis flashed on the screen.

It was well known that Merck Mercuriadis had connections to the Sicilian Mafia, or Cosa Nostra. He was a close associate of Francesco Guttadouro, nephew of Matteo Messina Denaro, who was also known as Diabolik—the last godfather of the Sicilian Mafia.

Cher clicked to the next slide, which showed a written language none of them had seen before. She explained that it was **Cruzeño or Isleno**, an extinct language once spoken by the Chumash people from the Channel Islands off the California coast. Cher then switched to another slide that displayed the translation of the message.

The words on the screen told the ancient myth of **Lewelew Demon**, also known as the riddling demon. According to the myth, the demon tested **Ciqneq**, the child of the clouds.

The riddle went like this:

"Here we are going to begin where you came from. Look to the south; we are seeing the Islands. We begin and see this island where it began, always it will continue. There goes one, two, three, four, five, six, seven—those who went to the west. Now, I am beginning; I don't know the end. I barely put my foot on land. Do you know we are under this sun and that you are seen by means of its light? It lies among the stars of the southern sky, the realm of the Axenpes (fly). I will dispose of all the flies and you, and take over your possessions."

This myth was the key to finding Christina and was clearly meant to mock Cher. It demonstrated how arrogant Merck Mercuriadis and the Hipgnosis Song Fund had become, believing themselves above the law and untouchable. Cher, having lived on the Malibu coast, was very familiar with the Chumash people. She had an old friend, **Julie Tumamait-Stenslie**, a Chumash elder and cultural resource consultant, who had helped decode and translate the myth they were now analyzing on the screen.

The information was entered into the Temptress Academy's supercomputer, which decoded seven riddles written after the myth. Each riddle needed to be interpreted to find a key, with seven locks holding Christina captive.

The first key's riddle, when translated, was as follows:

"Tadoussac pink granite rooftops of stainless steel don't stand idle to watch your neighbor bleed. Will not oppress a stranger. Consider

generations long past. Noah's ark, Hollywood red square, Bob Dylan's hideout, blowing in the wind. Can't play his guitar without this plectrum."

The riddle pointed to the **Skirball Cultural Center** in Los Angeles, a Jewish educational institute founded in 1996. The center was built with Tadoussac pink granite and stainless-steel rooftops and hosted exhibits, film events, and live performances. Among its exhibits was a collection dedicated to Bob Dylan, including his **double-0 Martin guitar**. The Temptress Academy's supercomputer was able to tap into Skirball's surveillance and security systems, where they discovered an x-ray of Dylan's guitar. Inside, lodged in the instrument, was a **plectrum** (guitar pick), which had slipped inside over time.

This guitar pick was the first key. However, retrieving it wouldn't be easy. The guitar was on display, behind glass, and protected by 24-hour surveillance and security guards. Gaining access would involve navigating a lot of red tape.

The riddle for the second key is translated as follows:

"From the black city where the elephant, hewn from basalt, sits. To the ragabo forest at the pianos, the planet moon on earth near the grotto of raspberries. You will need to gather molten pahoehoe. Be careful of Typhoon trapped below."

The landscape around **Mount Etna** in Sicily resembled a moonscape. **Piano Provenzana** was a winter ski resort, and **Piano delle Concazze** housed an observatory near the crater rim.

The **Grotto of Raspberries** referred to a cave formed by lava flows on Mount Etna, which is an active volcano with pahoehoe lava flows at its base. **Pahoehoe** is a smooth, ropy type of lava made up of thousands of small flow units called "toes." In Greek mythology, **Typhon**, a monstrous storm giant, was buried under Mount Etna by Zeus, causing the volcano's eruptions. To gather a "toe" from the lava was the second key.

The riddle for the third key is translated as follows:

"Sail past the two sirens to enchantress Morgana's underwater castle, Sickle City, the city built on the dead, a city without memory. You will need the blessings from the lady of the letter."

The two sirens referred to **Scylla and Charybdis**, located in the **Strait of Messina** between Sicily and Italy. Violent winds and clashing currents from the **Tyrrhenian** and **Ionian Seas** could reach speeds of 90 km/h, creating massive vortices. **Messina** was known as **Sickle City** (**Zancle**) due to its harbor's sickle-like shape. The harbor housed a statue of **Madonna della Lettera** (the Lady of the Letter).

Messina was said to be built on the dead due to the devastating earthquakes that had leveled it. Legend placed **Morgana's** underwater castle, home of the Arthurian villainess **Morgana Le Fey**, here. It was also said to be the final resting place of sailors whose ships had sunk in the strait.

The riddle for the fourth key is translated as follows:

"The promontory at the tip of the boot and the home of Scylla. The waves break on the mighty rocks with such a din, you can hear the

melodious voices of the mermaids sing. Charm of the myth that always returns to a whisper, enchanting the heart and soul. Curtain walls, towers, and loopholes, the exploits of Ulysses. Below the chapel and cisterns where the waves lap at its edge is a precious treasure chest where the whisper song lies."

This described the **Ruffo Castle** on the **Violet Coast**. The **Ruffo di Scilla Castle** stood at the tip of Italy's boot on the **Scilla Promontory**, a place of rare beauty overlooking the **Tyrrhenian Sea**. The town of **Scilla**, a fishing village with cobbled streets and pebble beaches, was straight out of myth. Below the castle, near its chapel and cisterns, lay the hidden treasure that held the whispering song mentioned in the riddle.

The riddle for the fifth key is translated as follows:

"Go past the chestnut woods and traces of old olive trees. Petrified three muses plundered, sculptured by a master of Gothic art. Pecten shells, bivalves, and the nymphs welcomed with music and dance steps. An ancient place of the Pleistocene era and pagan cults. Stalactite columns and calcite concretions, fossil shells set in the vault of caves like jewels. Gather the tears born from the stalactites."

This referred to the **Grotto di Tremusa**, the Tremusa caverns located in a secluded valley near **Scilla**, in the **Calabria** region of Italy. Drops of water - "tears" - falling from the stalactites were the key to be collected.

The riddle for the sixth key is translated as follows:

"Narrow brush strokes, wide brush strokes. Crushed by burden, underlying current. The magical Indian paintbrush, swirls and swirls. Black and gold petals, in all their glory, on what a host that golden bush. The magic flower of Enee-pah."

Even the supercomputer struggled to fully decode this riddle, but Cher's friend, **Julie Tumamait-Stenslie**, knew the story passed down through her Chumash ancestors about a **magic flower** on **Anacapa Island**, the only one of its kind. Julie also knew exactly where to find it.

The riddle for the seventh key is translated as follows:

"In the sacred sea of Kizh, where the blue dolphins swim, is the land of kings where the sand dunes cover and uncover the dead. The wind, the ravens, the sea elephants, and the sea lions are still there. A

luxurious cape of sealskin and feathers, lost to the Vatican. Footprints in the sand lead to grooved petroglyphs and whale effigies. Here lies the too-shout stone that sings."

This referred to **San Nicolas Island**, one of the Channel Islands off the coast of California. The **Cave of Whales** on the island contains petroglyphs and pictographs resembling killer whales. **San Nicolas** is where the **Chumash** produced the **magician's stones** (known as too-shout stones). **Scott O'Dell's** novel *Island of the Blue Dolphins* tells the story of a girl who lived on the island alone for eighteen years after the Spanish removed the Chumash to mainland missions, but she was left behind. A beautiful **cape of sealskin and feathers**, once belonging to the **Kizh people**, had been taken and presented to the Vatican, but it was subsequently lost.

The Song of Seven Languages: Once they had gathered all the items (Keys) from the riddles to unlock the seven locks, a final riddle emerged. It involved using the items to access the *Song of Seven Languages*, which was necessary to free Christina from her state of probability. The song would also reveal Christina's location. The translated riddle read:

"Seven Keys for seven locks. Fires turned the white condor black. Pass through the waterfalls. The colorful patterns shimmer in twilight. Violinist Max Mendel plays Bach. The ghost of Cabrillo waits for you there, to give you the Song of Seven Languages and the map."

On *Santa Cruz Island*, off the California coast, lies the *Painted Cave*, which can only be accessed by water. During the rainy season, a waterfall cascades over the mouth of the cave.

It is the second-largest sea cave in the U.S., with an entrance over 130 feet high. The Chumash people believe this is where they were created, calling the island *Limmu*. Evidence suggests human presence on the Channel Islands for over 13,000 years. The name *Santa Cruz* was given after a Spanish expedition left behind a staff topped with an iron cross. When the Chumash returned the staff the next day, the island was marked as *La Isla de la Santa Cruz* (Holy Cross) on a 1770 exploration map.

Violinist *Max Mandel* once performed and recorded music in the Painted Cave. One legend, often shared around campfires, tells of *Juan Rodriguez Cabrillo*, the first European to explore the West Coast. He is said to have died from an infected sea lion bite while exploring the

Painted Cave. On his deathbed, Cabrillo reportedly asked to be buried in the cave so he could haunt the sea lions. His grave has never been found.

Taking the Keys (items from the riddles) to the Painted Cave and making offerings there would provide access to the *Song of Seven Languages* and a map revealing Christina's location.

The *Cleopatra*, awarded by the *Temptress Academy*, was the most prestigious music industry award. A miniature golden sculpture of Cleopatra, holding a ruby rose in one hand and a turquoise papyrus scepter in the other, was given to the best performer each year.

To retrieve the Keys, the team decided to hold a *music competition* at the venues where the Keys were hidden. This would serve as a distraction for their adversaries. They invited musicians to compete for the Cleopatra Award and planned to select seven musicians to sing the Song of Seven Languages, which needed to be sung in seven different languages. Meanwhile, Andrea Stolpe and the songwriters could search for the Keys.

The first venue was the *Ziegler Amphitheatre* at the Skirball Cultural Center, where the first Key was located. North American, South American, and Australian musicians would perform here. The European musicians would be invited to compete at the *Ruffo Castle of Scilla* in Calabria, Italy, coinciding with an annual jazz festival held in the castle's courtyard.

The semi-finalists from both locations would then continue the competition at the *Banana Festival* in *Port Hueneme, California,* located near the Channel Islands, where the remaining Keys were hidden.

A CELEBRATION OF A DIVERSE WORKING PORT

Once all seven Keys were obtained and seven finalists selected, they would join Andrea Stolpe, the songwriters, and the Chumash in venturing to *Santa Cruz Island*. Together, they would pass through the waterfall into the Painted Cave, make offerings of the seven Keys, and obtain the map that would lead them to Christina and the *Song of Seven Languages*, which would finally free her.

The team sent out invitations to musicians, each arriving in a scroll sealed with the Temptress Academy's emblem. Inside, a poster provided all the essential details about the upcoming competition.

Joel burst through the door of the Chateau Motel Recording Studio, waving a scroll frantically. "It's on, it's on, it's on!" he panted, shoving the scroll into Jeremy's face.

Jeremy glared at him before snatching the scroll out of Joel's hand. His eyes lit up the moment he saw the Temptress Academy's seal.

Jeremy Buck and the Bang—his band, which included Joel Geiss and Christopher Hannah—knew they'd have to be at the top of their game. But with their reputation for unforgettable live performances, they were confident. As AI continued to integrate into the music scene, Jeremy's background as an advanced audio engineer and producer gave him an edge. An Andrea Stolpe alumnus, he often collaborated with her and other songwriters, especially in their investigations into deepfake technology.

Jeremy knew his friend and rival, Adam Levine, and his band Maroon 5 would be invited as well. They always had a friendly competition, much like the one Blake Shelton and Adam had on *The Voice*. Jeremy liked to call Adam "Jonah Pouski" because neither of them liked the name, which was exactly the point. Jeremy would send for Flash, the band's truck driver, a drifter from Canada.

Adam Levine slammed his fist on the desk. "Jimmo!" he yelled. "Get me another drink!" His lips curled into a menacing frown as he clutched the Temptress Academies scroll in his hand. When Jimmo brought him his Mai Tai—Adam had been enjoying them all afternoon out by the pool—he barked at him to get his act together and load the music equipment into the semi-trailer. "Immediately," Adam snapped. They would be heading to the Ziegler Amphitheater at the Skirball Cultural Center in Los Angeles.

Jimmo paid little attention to Adam, knowing his bark was worse than his bite. He took Adam's comments with a grain of salt. Adam was a great person to work with, and his demeanor was always lighthearted, often accompanied by a sense of humor. A smirk crossed Adam's face as he sipped his Mai Tai, thinking about the upcoming competition with Jeremy Buck. He knew for sure that Jeremy would be there, and Adam couldn't wait to teach him a thing or two about music.

With the growing threats of artificial intelligence, cyberattacks, and sabotage from rival music labels against the Temptress Academy, the competition would be filled with challenges. Even bands not included in the competition would harbor grudges. It would be up to Andrea Stolpe and the songwriters to ensure the contestants' safety from these external threats.

Meanwhile, Jeremy, Joel, and Christopher were busy loading up the semi-van trailer. Their driver, Flash, was already on his way. The trailer had two compartments: the front one for the band members and crew, complete with a kitchen, lounge area, bunk beds, and a bathroom; the back compartment housed the equipment. Flash was a seasoned professional truck driver, having built ice roads in the north, driven across the Delta Ice Road through Yellowknife Bay, and navigated the British Columbia Rockies, including the Coquihalla and Crowsnest Pass. He had also worked in the Alberta oilfields, driving off-road through muskegs and swamps, where chaining up was essential.

Their destination was the Ziegler Amphitheater at the Skirball Cultural Center, northwest of Beverly Hills. The competition would feature heavy hitters like Pink, Bruno Mars, Dave Matthews, Luke Combs, Lady Gaga, Lou Reed, Maroon 5, the Foo Fighters, Jonas Brothers, Shannon and the Clams, Kelly Clarkson, and more. There would also be Latin bands such as Flor Amargo, Mon Laferte, Diego Verdaguer, Manuel Garcia, Julieta Venegas, Lila Downs, Shakira, Australian artists like Jessica Mauboy, Nick Cave, Kylie Minogue, Sia, and Canadians like Drake and Bryan Adams.

Meanwhile, the European bands would convene in Messina, Sicily. From there, they would board a ferry across the Strait of Messina to Scilla, Italy, and the Castello Ruffo di Scilla (Ruffo Castle). The European competition participants included from France: Zaz, Joseph Kamel, and Maelle; from Germany: Sarah Lesch and Joakim Witt; from Austria: Mojo Blues Band; from Switzerland: Hillbilly Moon Explosion; from Spain: Fito & Fitipaldis, Café Quijano, Celtas Cortos, and Mikel Erentxum; from Italy: Adriano Celentano, Laura Pausini, and Negrita; from the UK: Kitty, Daisy and Louis, Emilia Clarke, and the Waterboys; from Croatia: Crvena Jubuka; from Bosnia: Dino Merlin; from Serbia: Riblja Čorba and Đorđe Balašević; from Belgium: Vaya Con Dios; from Latvia: Ducele; from Montenegro: Vanja Radovanović (Vanja, the nephew of Miladin Sobić).

Dražen Žera Žerić was in his recording studio in Zagreb, Croatia, practicing with his band when he received the Temptress Academy's scroll. Dražen was the frontman of Crvena Jabuka (translated as Red Apple). Although the band originated in Sarajevo, Bosnia and Herzegovina, it had been based in Zagreb since the Yugoslav Wars. Dražen, along with Tomislav, Krešimir, Darko, and Igor, would leave Zagreb for Pula Harbor, a three-hour drive away, and from there board a ship to Messina, Sicily.

Bora Đorđević, the frontman of the band Riblja Čorba (translated as Fish Soup), also received a Temptress scroll. Bora had been a controversial figure over the years but was known as a gifted musician, songwriter, and poet. His political stance had often caused trouble for the band. One of their most memorable songs, "All Quiet on the Western Front," was a non-aligned anthem criticizing both Western and Soviet ideals. It still resonated today. Bora, along with Vicko, Vidoja, and Nikola, would leave Belgrade for Dubrovnik and sail from there to Messina.

Zaz was in her apartment in the heart of Montmartre, close to the Sacré-Cœur. In her winter garden of the 1950s-era building, she received her scroll. Zaz and her band would take the TGV high-speed train from Paris to Milan, Italy, and then the Frecciarossa train to Rome, with stops in Bologna and Florence. Once in Rome, they would board a ship to Messina.

Sarah Lesch was teaching a music class at Eberhard Karls University in Tübingen when the school secretary burst in. "Sarah! Sarah!" she exclaimed, interrupting the class as she handed Sarah the scroll. It was Sarah's invitation to the Temptress Academy's competition for the Golden Sculpture of Cleopatra, the highest honor in the music industry. The secretary, Miss Tiavicho, was overjoyed for Sarah, knowing how much this opportunity meant to her. Miss Tiavicho had already begun booking Sarah's travel plans. She and the band would take the Deutsche Bahn ICE 619 train to Munich via Stuttgart, and from there, the OBB Nightjet (NJ295) to Rome. From Rome they would also take a ship to Messina. The other European bands would all take similar routes to get to Messina. There would be a member of Andrea Stolpe and the songwriters that would travel with each of the musicians to their destination.

With the growing threats of artificial intelligence, cyberattacks, and sabotage from rival music labels against the Temptress Academy, the competition would be filled with challenges. Even bands not included in the competition would harbor grudges. It would be up to Andrea Stolpe and the songwriters to ensure the contestants' safety from these external threats.

However, trouble was already brewing. Flor Amarso was missing. When Flor and the mariachi band, along with her mother, arrived at the U.S. border, Flor went through customs first. But when her mother and the mariachi band attempted to pass through, a guard whispered something to the customs agent, who then turned them back. Flor was not allowed to turn around and join them, leaving her stranded. Flor's mother, sick with worry, contacted Cher at the Temptress Academy.

Cher immediately suspected foul play and sent Andrea and the team to the border to get the mariachi band and Flor's mother through customs and locate Flor.

When Flor left the customs border crossing, she still had her guitar and the Temptress Academy scroll. As she walked along the parking lot that connected to the highway, she pondered her next steps. Near the end of the lot, there was an older blue truck—or what was left of it. The truck's blue paint had worn away, leaving a patchwork of rust and faded blue. The truck had a flatbed deck, with locked cages full of chickens.

An older Mexican gentleman stood next to the truck, his graying hair tucked under a light brown velvet cowboy hat with sweat stains around the brim. He fiddled with the straps securing the cages. He smiled and greeted Flor with a cheerful "Hola" as she approached. Flor, unsure of what else to do, asked if he could give her a ride and where he was headed.

The man introduced himself as Emiliano Carlos Gustaro, and he was driving up the Pacific Coast Highway to a ranch near Malibu Colony called the Big Heart Ranch, a working animal sanctuary. He kindly offered her a ride.

When Emiliano and Flor arrived at the ranch, Flor was surprised to learn it was both a sanctuary for rescued farm animals and a community wellness center. Emiliano was donating the chickens to the ranch, as years ago, the ranch had helped his daughter, a domestic violence survivor, and Emiliano had never forgotten their kindness.

After a pleasant meal on the veranda with Nora, the president of the ranch, Flor was given a guided tour of the farm. The sanctuary housed horses, donkeys, pigs, goats, alpacas, deer, bunnies, and, of course, chickens. Once the tour was complete, Emiliano and Flor headed back toward the highway.

As Emiliano made his way south toward Mexico, Flor decided it was time to part ways. He dropped her off at an intersection before turning onto the Pacific Coast Highway to head back the way they had come. Flor began walking north and, after a while, came to a bridge crossing Malibu Creek, which flowed into Malibu Lagoon.

Flor, wary of attracting attention after her experience at the border, veered off the highway and down beside the creek, where large boulders lined the shore. She discovered a few wooden crates, one of which contained nylon tarps. She used the tarps to set up a makeshift camp nestled between the boulders.

In an effort to stay under the radar, Flor decided to disguise herself as a boy. Over the next few days, she crossed the highway and walked down to the historic Adamson House near Malibu Surfrider Beach. With her guitar in hand, she busked for tips to cover her meals. The people were friendly, and although they didn't pay much attention to her beyond appreciating her music, the tips were enough.

Some evenings, after busking, Flor would walk down to the shore, sit on the rocks, and gaze out at the ocean, reflecting on what to do next. She hummed a song, thinking of her mom and the mariachi band:

These tears I shed,

This might be it, might be my last gasp.
Have no chance, waiting for the fall,
What if I run out of breath,
What if I miss my step?
The mariachi will come save me,
The mariachi will come save me,
We will dance to the music,
My mother and me,
And know joy.

Meanwhile, Andrea Stolpe and the songwriters were an integral part of the Temptress Academy. They didn't just protect the artists and musicians—they collaborated with them, co-writing songs and contributing to melodies, harmony, rhythm, and form. Before Andrea and the team departed, Cher informed Andrea of a last-minute change in plans. While some songwriters had already been contacted to join various bands, Cher had received information about potential trouble in Messina, and Andrea and Lumina were urgently needed there. Myles and Madison would continue the mission in North America, assisting with getting Flor's mother and the mariachi band through customs, finding Flor, and supervising the other songwriters overseeing musicians going to the Ziegler Amphitheater at Skirball.

Trouble at Skirball

The search for Flor continued, as did the effort to get Flor's mother and the mariachi band across the border. Meanwhile, the competition at the Skirball Center was starting. The cultural center and museum closed at 5 p.m., but the amphitheater remained open until 11 p.m. for the competition.

Myles and Madison were at the Skirball Center, having sent Tyler and Angela to the border to assist Flor's mom and the mariachi band. Others were dispatched to search for Flor. They entered the museum just before closing and hid in the coatroom until the lights went out and everyone had left. The security guard made his rounds every hour, returning to his office to monitor the cameras. The second guard stayed outside, walking the grounds and occasionally chatting with the office guard.

Once the inside guard passed the coatroom and disappeared down the hall, Myles and Madison snuck out and made their way toward the Bob Dylan exhibit. The Temptress Academy's supercomputer had hacked into the security system, concealing their movements from the cameras. At the Dylan exhibit, where Bob Dylan's double-O Martin guitar was on display, Madison kept watch while Myles climbed over the rope barrier.

The guitar was housed behind glass doors, Myles slid open the doors and took the guitar down from the case, when Myles gently shook the guitar he could hear something rattling inside. Turning the guitar upside down, he shook it a few more times until a guitar pick fell to the floor. He picked it up, slipped it into his pocket, and returned the guitar to its display, closing the glass doors.

Myles and Madison then retraced their steps toward the coatroom and the exit. Halfway down the hall, a loud noise startled them—it was music. Part of the Bob Dylan exhibit featured an interactive display where visitors could play instruments along with Dylan's song "Blowing in the Wind." But no one was there. This was no coincidence; someone had activated the system, triggering alarms. The security guard would soon be headed their way.

Myles and Madison bolted back into the coatroom. There, Myles quickly slid a chair underneath a window, climbed on top, and opened it. He popped the screen out, stepped down, and helped Madison up onto the chair.

Madison crawled out of the window, with Myles right behind her. They tumbled onto the grass, trying to make as little noise as possible. In the distance, they could see the outside security guard, flashlight in hand, moving toward them. The inside security guard would also be approaching soon. They were trapped.

Just as they were about to be spotted by the outside guard, a ruckus erupted to their right, where a row of shrubs lined a pathway. It was Jeremy Buck and Adam Levine, both visibly drunk. Adam had started singing along to Dylan's song playing from the museum, and Jeremy taunted him for being too high-pitched, saying it sounded like he was wearing a skirt. Adam, not missing a beat, retorted that it wasn't a skirt—it was a kilt.

Meanwhile, Jeremy began singing, "Nothing under the skirt, left it all blowin' in the wind, up on the stage giving the fans an eyeful," then pretended to gag. The distraction was enough to divert the security guard's attention, allowing Madison and Myles to slip away into the night. They didn't get far before they both burst into laughter, nearly to the point of tears. They had the first key.

The legend of the strait of Messina:

Sailing too close to Calabria, the point at the tip of the boot of Italy, meant passing Scylla—a sailor-snatching sea-nymph with twelve feet and six heads on long, snaky necks. Each head had triple rows of shark-like teeth, and their loins were girded by baying dogs that lived in a cave on the rocky shore. On the other side of the strait, too close to Sicily, lay Charybdis, a whirlpool with a mouth that could swallow an entire ship. She was the daimon of the tides, her thrice-daily sucking and expulsion of waters causing idioms like "between a rock and a hard place," or "between the devil and the deep blue sea"— expressions born from choosing between equally dangerous extremes that inevitably lead to disaster.

Bora emerged from his cabin and made his way to the bridge. They were heading into the Strait of Messina, and the captain had called for him. The skies had darkened ominously, and the waters were churning violently. The currents pulled in different directions.

The captain asked Bora if they should turn back, but Bora dismissed the suggestion. He insisted on pushing forward toward the port of Messina to stay on schedule for the competition. As they neared the port, the waters grew even rougher. Other ships heading into Messina Harbor were visibly struggling to navigate, tossed violently by the waves. Among them was Drazen's ship and the Crvena Jubuka group, including Zaz and Sara Lesch's ships, along with other musicians' vessels.

Sarah looked out the window of the cockpit. The first mate had called the quartermaster to help at the helm, as the wheel was slipping from his grasp with each lunge of the boat, diving into the troughs of waves before surging up onto the next crest. The black clouds were thick with electricity, and lightning crackled in every direction. Zaz's ship was nearby, and she could see the waves growing enormous, crashing onto the shoreline before their ship dropped back between them, only for everything to go black. Zaz thought she might be sick and made her way to her cabin.

Bora peered over the portside of the ship, noticing strange fish surfacing in the waves. Some were atrophied, their eyes protruding from their heads, others bioluminescent. The ships around them now seemed to be suspended in mid-air, some even upside down, floating as if weightless. It was fata morgana. One ship, appearing to fall from the sky, seemed ready to crash into Bora's vessel—the Flying Dutchman. It felt like a bad omen.

When Andrea and Lumina flew into Messina's airspace, they were horrified by the destruction below. The waves were towering, spinning ships around like toys. Whirlpools formed in every direction. They had boarded a helicopter in Naples, bringing all their equipment with them. The computer screens flashed with alarms and codes. This storm was no natural phenomenon—it was being generated by AI.

Andrea needed to access the search engines to pinpoint the source of the interference, decode it, and shut it down—or at least jam the magnetic fields amplifying the atmosphere. She suspected powerful electromagnets were being used, though she wasn't sure if their onboard computers were strong enough to counteract them. As soon as the download began, the winds intensified drastically, and whoever was behind this interference was aware of Andrea's attempt to stop it.

The helicopter began losing tail rotor authority, and the pilot executed a near-perfect autorotation, though it was only a temporary fix. The winds were shifting violently, making it clear they wouldn't be able to download the necessary data fast enough. The helicopter spiraled out of control, and Andrea glanced down at the harbor. The seawall was crumbling as the earth split, forming cracks that spread toward the city—an earthquake.

In the midst of this chaos, Andrea saw the golden lady statue perched on a tall column in the harbor. To her horror, the statue began to stretch and expand toward the sky. It grew larger and larger, and its face shifted, with a sigh of relief Andrea realized it was Cher—the Temptress, now using the supercomputer from the academy to override the threat.

As the winds began to subside and the helicopter steadied, Andrea's download completed. The lightning slowed, and the waves and whirlpools calmed. They were safe, and the city was safe.

Bora, looking over the bow of the ship, saw Drazen standing on the deck of his ship. They exchanged a wave as they headed toward port.

Zaz and Sarah's ships were also making their way to the harbor. Together, they now held the fifth key, as Cher had invoked the *Stella Madonna della Lettera* (the Lady of the Letter) and summoned her blessings. "We bless you and the city," she declared. All the ships and musicians arrived safely.

The next morning, some of Andrea Stolpe's team, Tom and Angela, left Messina. Tom had escorted Sarah from Germany, and Angela had brought Zaz from France. They boarded a train to the ancient port city of Catania, located at the foot of Mount Edna. It was still early when they arrived at the Catania Centrale train station, so Tom suggested they take a cab to La Pescheria fish market in the heart of the city.

The fish market was alive with energy. Stallholders shouted prices, haggled with customers, and exchanged playful barbs. At the entrance stood an Amerano marble fountain, with a terrace overlooking the market—a sensory overload.

Tom and Angela descended the lava stone steps and joined the crowd. They passed giant swordfish heads next to bright pink cuts of fish, piles of octopus next to buckets of snails, crates of oysters, and gleaming trays of squid, prawns, and more varieties of fish than they could count. The market spilled into narrow streets lined with fruit and vegetable stalls. Oranges, lemons, artichokes, and eggplants were piled high, along with mushrooms, dried fruits, dates, and nuts. The legacy of the Arab occupation of Sicily was evident in the spices, and prepared antipasto, including freshly grilled artichokes and red peppers, their skins charred black and seasoned with vinegar, salt, and olive oil.

Tom and Angela picked out a few items and sat on a bench, enjoying a picnic lunch with warm ciabatta bread. Tom had arranged for a guide, and it wasn't long before Tracy arrived to take them to the north side of Mount Edna, to the Piano Provenzana. They drove on the A18 freeway, exiting at Fiumefreddo di Scilla and continuing to Linguaglossa. From there, they turned onto Via Umberto, following signs for Etna Nord. The drive through hairpin bends and lush vegetation offered stunning views of the surrounding landscape.

Piano Provenzana was a ski resort in winter, but in the summer, it served as a hub for hiking and mountain biking. From here, they continued through hazel groves and pine forests up to Piano delle Con Cazze, the volcano observatory at 2825 meters above sea level. They hiked another five kilometers past old lava flows and extinct craters, eventually reaching the summit crater of Mount Edna at 3300 meters.

The hike was challenging, with vertigo-inducing climbs and thick fog, but they made it to the summit. After stopping to catch their breath, Tom realized that Tracy had disappeared. He had intentionally left them on the mountain. However, Tom wasn't concerned. They had all the necessary equipment, including a satellite phone, GPS radio, and mountaineering gear.

The restricted areas around the crater were off-limits, but Tom and Angela needed to get closer to the lava flows. Using Google Maps on his iPad, Tom found a narrow path leading down into the crater. They followed it, crossing a lava plain with volcano cones and steam rising from cracks. The warmth from the crater contrasted sharply with the cold winds at the summit. They entered a lava flow tunnel and, through the steam, saw an orange, glowing lava flow.

Tom carefully retrieved a chunk of lava with specialized tongs and placed it into a case designed for the purpose. On the way out, Angela noticed something odd—what looked like raspberries growing from the cracks in the black lava. She approached, and to her amazement, saw the largest, plumpest raspberries she had ever seen. They tasted delicious.

As they crossed the lava plain and started up the narrow path leading to the summit, they reached the steepest part of the trail. The ledge was narrow, with a substantial drop on one side and a sheer cliff face on the other. Tom and Angela paused, hearing a scraping noise followed by small pebbles and gravel rolling down the path toward them. Suddenly, a large boulder came tumbling down. Tom yelled at Angela to look out as he dodged the boulder, which rolled past her. Angela clung to the cliff face as it passed.

More boulders came crashing down, and Tom looked up, realizing Tracy was pushing them from the top of the ridge. There wasn't much they could do but try to avoid the rocks as they kept tumbling down. As Tracy sent another massive boulder toward the edge—one that neither Tom nor Angela would be able to dodge—something unexpected happened. Tracy was suddenly airborne, screaming as he flew past them, bouncing off the jagged cliff before disappearing into the chasm below.

Tom and Angela scrambled to the top of the ridge. There, standing at the summit, was a billy goat—either a Messinese or an Argentata dell'Etna, both domestic breeds known in the area. It must have been the goat that had punted Tracy off the ledge. As they watched, the goat wandered off and disappeared down the trail.

Someone had hired Tracy to sabotage them, but nature had intervened—perhaps Zeus himself was looking down on them. Tracy had hidden the jeep, but Tom and Angela made their way back to Piano Provenzana, where they caught a tour bus back to Catania. From there, they took the return train to Messina, and they now had the second key.

Upon arriving in Messina, Tom and Angela simply had to switch trains. Andrea, along with the songwriters and musicians, was heading to Scilla and the Ruffo Castle. This particular train had a unique feature: it would be loaded in two parts onto a ferry to cross the Strait of Messina. While the process was slow, it provided a perfect opportunity to relax and enjoy the stunning scenery on such a beautiful day.

Ruffo Castle overlooked the Tyrrhenian Sea and the Aeolian Islands, with the quaint fishing village of Chianlea nestled at its feet. On the southern side, the Violet Coast met the beautiful Marina Grande di Scilla basin beach.

When they arrived at the castle, Andrea and Lumina immediately set out in search of the entrance to the cellar hidden deep within the castle. At first, there seemed to be no way down, but as Andrea explored beneath the grand staircase, she noticed one section appeared older— much older. This part of the castle had once been a monastery in the 9th century, later expanded by the Romans for fortifications. Andrea suspected the wall in question was from that era.

Kneeling down to inspect further, Andrea noticed a crack running the length of one stone block. She brushed away the dust to reveal a fine crack that encircled the entire block. It was dark under the staircase, so Andrea took out her cell phone and switched on the flashlight. On the block with the crack, two small outcroppings—like tabs—were visible at the corners. At the base of the block, faint markings scratched into the stone hinted that something had been moved across the floor. Just above the block, similar faint markings appeared.

Andrea wet her fingers with her water bottle and patted the markings. As she did, barely visible letters emerged: ancient Greek letters spelling "Daughter of Crataeis." She felt along the block, brushing her hand across one of the outcroppings. When she pushed, she heard a barely audible click. The block seemed to shift slightly. Pushing harder, a grating sound followed, and the block began to swing open, revealing a narrow gap.

Lumina crawled into the space beside her, and together, they managed to push the block further until it swung wide enough for them to crawl through. On the other side, they found a small landing with stone steps leading downward. As Andrea shone her flashlight into the space, she felt a cool draft and smelled the salty scent of seawater.

Lumina followed her down the spiraling steps. After descending a dozen steps, they heard the same grating sound they had heard when opening the block. Lumina dashed back up the stairs to check. When the flashlight illuminated the block, they saw it had closed back to its original position. No matter how hard they tried to push it open, it wouldn't budge. They had no choice but to continue down the steps.

The stairs were steep and crumbling in places, and Andrea nearly slipped several times. After what felt like hundreds of steps, they reached a cavern. The walls glistened with moisture, sparkling in the flashlight's beam. Moving forward, they came upon a large gap in one of the walls about twenty yards ahead. As they approached, they saw it was a tunnel entrance that dropped steeply into darkness.

Beyond the tunnel, they could make out two stone steps leading up to a platform. On the platform stood a stone table, and as they neared, the faint sound of what seemed like a dog whimpering reached their ears. Stepping onto the platform, they saw the stone table had a ledge running along it. Nestled inside a square slot on the ledge was a ceramic tablet with writing on it. The whimpering noise grew louder, soon transforming into yelping.

Suddenly, shadows in the darkness shifted, and Andrea's flashlight illuminated the tail of a snake slithering across the stone floor. Then, a terrifying canine head with rows of gleaming teeth appeared in the light. More heads followed, and the yelping grew into high-pitched howls as the beasts snapped their jaws. It was Scylla, the sea monster from legend.

For a brief moment, Andrea and Lumina froze in fear. But as Andrea stepped back, she accidentally pushed against the stone table, dislodging the ceramic tablet. The monster let out an earsplitting shriek and lunged toward them. Its half-dozen canine heads darted at them from all directions. Without hesitation, Andrea and Lumina leaped off the platform and ran toward the steps.

They had no chance of making it to the spiral staircase in time—the creature was on top of them, its snapping jaws mere inches from their backs. With no other option, they both dove into the dark tunnel they had passed earlier. They tumbled down the shaft, narrowly avoiding one of the canine jaws, which snapped just behind Lumina. As they fell, the tunnel eventually leveled out, and they came to a stop, tangled in a heap.

After gathering themselves, they crawled forward, the tunnel narrowing as they went. Soon, they were on their hands and knees. Andrea was certain the sea monster was a hologram, set up by Merk Mercudiadas and the hypnosis group. They continued crawling until they reached what appeared to be a dead end. The surface felt soft, and Andrea could push her hands into the soil, which was loose and aerated, likely close to the surface.

As they cleared away the soil, faint light began to filter through. They soon broke free from the earth and emerged into the fresh air, surrounded by blooming strawberry trees. The scent of the flowers was invigorating after the musty air of the cavern.

They found themselves on a cliff face, towering a hundred feet or more above the ground. Above them, the canopy of trees stretched hundreds of yards. Far in the distance, they glimpsed the top of a campanile—the bell tower of the Maria Santissima Church, opposite Ruffo Castle. They were in a gorge between the two landmarks, with no choice but to make their way through the thick vegetation toward the church.

They struggled up the cliffside, grabbing roots and branches for support, inching upward, exhausted but determined. About a third of the way up, Andrea reached for a ledge, but as she grabbed the dirt and roots, the earth gave way, and she slipped, dangling from the edge. Lumina scrambled up to help, pulling her onto the ledge. They paused to catch their breath, surveying the steep drop below.

The ledge they rested on was small—about a meter by two meters—but it offered a brief respite as they continued their grueling climb.

Andrea stared at the ledge from which she had removed the soil and vegetation. It didn't seem natural anymore. The stone surface had been chiseled smooth and polished—it was man-made. Curiosity tugged at her, and she began pulling away more of the overgrowth, revealing faint etchings in the stone. To her amazement, intricate patterns and designs were chiseled into the surface, along with strange script.

As they cleared away more of the vegetation, Andrea's eyes widened in disbelief. She leaned closer, studying the symbols. "It can't be," she murmured, her breath hitching in her chest. A rush of adrenaline flooded through her body, but she couldn't catch her breath.

Andrea and Lumina glanced around nervously, as though they feared being watched. But soon, they realized there was no way anyone could see them. It was impossible. The whole discovery was simply too incredible to comprehend.

Andrea rubbed her eyes, trying to convince herself it was all just her imagination. Given the earthquakes and upheavals in the land, it made sense that this place had remained hidden. Maybe that was the intention all along. From here, the view over the sea and horizon was spectacular. The question lingered—did they dare share this with the world? Or was it better to keep it a secret? After a moment of contemplation, they decided to cover the stone back up for now.

The further they ventured into the gorge, the more Andrea realized there was no cell service, and their phone batteries had long since drained. It was as if time itself had slipped away. A full day must have passed since they entered the cavern. With no other option, they began the long, arduous climb up the cliff. For hours, they painstakingly worked their way up, grabbing onto roots and branches, sometimes dangling perilously over the edge as they scrambled up the steep incline.

As Andrea climbed, her mind wandered back to the crypt they had uncovered. It was clear now—it had been the lid of a crypt. The landscape had changed so drastically, ravaged by earthquakes, landslides, and tsunamis, that it had swallowed the crypt, hiding it away for who knew how long. But now, the question remained—did the world need to know about this?

By the time they emerged from the dense foliage, dusk had settled. They were back at the rear of the Church of Maria Santissima. A group of tourists from Amsterdam were taking pictures near the church, and they kindly lent Andrea and Lumina a cell phone. After a quick call and a short wait, Mark and Jan, some of the songwriters, arrived in a rental car to pick them up. Andrea had managed to slip the ceramic tablet into her backpack, the fourth key.

While Andrea and Lumina had been in the cavern, the rest of the group—Tom, Angela, Tyler, and Crystal—had left for the Tremusa Caverns to search for the Tears of the Stalactites, the fifth key. From Scilla, they headed to the village of Melia, situated on the plateau. From there, a single paved road crossed the plain, gradually descending into a valley. The remnants of old olive trees lined the path, and a trail led down to a portal. However, the trail had fallen into disrepair—the railing was broken, and some of the posts had fallen, making the path a bit challenging.

The area felt eerily isolated. As Angela and Crystal stepped into the entrance of the portal, they exchanged a glance and shivered. The chamber to the left was much larger than the one on the right, and they had to stoop to enter. Tom and Tyler had brought flashlights to navigate through the darkness.

They moved further into the dark cavern, flashlights cutting through the gloom. The limestone walls shimmered with fossils, so abundant in places they made the rocks appear like piles of shells. As Tom swept his flashlight along the cavern walls, the girls let out a shriek and clutched each other in terror. Tom's light had landed on three short, translucent figures resembling females, their whitish forms contrasted by large, black eyes.

The ghostly figures emitted an ear-piercing screech as their mouths, or where their mouths should have been, opened into black voids. A gust of wind materialized from nowhere, sending specks of dust swirling into the faces of the four intruders. Tom stumbled backward, as did Tyler, while Angela and Crystal dropped to their knees, holding each other tightly. The three spectral figures began to expand, their screams growing louder, reverberating off the cavern walls.

Tyler, who had dropped his flashlight in his panic, scrambled back toward the entrance with Angela and Crystal. It seemed as though one of the figures was poised to devour him. Tom, acting quickly, retrieved an emergency flare from his pack—something he had kept from their trek up Mount Edra. He removed the cap, struck the flint against the cavern wall, and a brilliant white light erupted with a hiss and crackle. The ghostly images vanished instantly, leaving behind only silence and the flare's sharp sparkling.

Tyler regained his footing and pulled out a glass tube from his pack, carefully collecting drops of water from a stalactite. Once they were back in the sunshine, Angela and Crystal both sighed in relief. They had the fifth key and began their return to Scilla and Ruffo Castle.

By the time Mark and Jan arrived at Ruffo Castle with Andrea and Lumina, having picked them up from the Church of Maria Santissima, the night's final performance was underway. Zaz was captivating the crowd with her song, *Je Veux*. Tom, Angela, Tyler, and Crystal returned just in time to catch the show.

The last day of their stay in Scilla offered a chance for relaxation and exploration. The musicians and songwriters enjoyed the remnants of towers, dungeons, and battlements, the lighthouse, and a small museum at Ruffo Castle. They marveled at the lush hills and azure seas, basking in Scilla's near-tropical climate—a rarity in mainland Europe.

Their exploration led them to the Church of Maria Santissima Immaculata, a structure twice destroyed by earthquakes but magnificently rebuilt. Inside, they admired artistic masterpieces, particularly the majestic wall mosaic depicting an angel illuminating

Chianalea di Scilla and a 17th-century statue of the Immaculate Conception.

Next, they visited Spiaggia di Scilla, a beach lined with bars and a charming promenade with palms in the Marina Grande area. The golden sands mixed with gravel, pastel-colored houses, and steep alleyways created a postcard-perfect scene. From Marina Grande, they walked through a small coastal tunnel to Chianalea, the historic fishing village. There, narrow cobbled streets and sea-lapped houses gave way to canals and fishing boats. Naturally, they indulged in Scilla's famed swordfish panini at Civico 5, reputedly the birthplace of this local delicacy.

Later, they took the elevator from Marina Grande to the Belvedere of Piazza San Rocco. The panoramic view of Scilla was breathtaking. After a day of relaxation and sightseeing, the group boarded a train to Reggio Calabria Airport.

The competition's finalists—Zaz, Sarah, Bora, and Drazen—would continue to Los Angeles and then to Port Hueneme. The rest of the musicians, though headed in separate directions, left grateful for the experience and wishing the finalists the best of luck. Andrea Stolpe and the songwriters, along with the Temptress Academy, had secured the first five keys. Now, only two remained, and their next destination was the Channel Islands off California's coast.

When Myles and Madison returned to the Ziegler Amphitheater, Shannon and the Clams were on stage, performing *I Need You Bad*.

The crowd was enthralled, waving their phone lights and singing along. But the atmosphere shifted abruptly as a commotion erupted at the back of the crowd. The crash of cymbals was followed by pounding drums and blaring horns, loud enough to halt the performance.

It was the Hipgnosis Henchmen Regiment—a marching band seemingly dispatched by Merck Mercuriadis to sabotage the competition. Dressed in long trench coats, dark face masks, and helmets with dramatic plumes, the henchmen were out of sync as they marched, raising their arms in a grotesque parody of the Sieg Heil salute. The crowd jeered and booed, giving them thumbs down. Even Shannon, up on stage, flipped them off and shouted curses.

Amid the chaos, Adam and Jeremy stumbled to the front of the stage. Spotting an emergency fire hose, they turned it on and aimed it at the approaching henchmen. A stream of water blasted into the intruders, knocking them over as their instruments clattered to the ground. The crowd erupted in cheers, pelting the henchmen with whatever they could find.

The scene devolved into mayhem, with Adam and Jeremy gleefully soaking the henchmen, sending them sprawling with every powerful jet of water. Security intervened and called the police, escalating the spectacle as the henchmen scrambled to retreat.

The police had started moving into the crowd, shields and batons in hand, threatening to fire tear gas and smoke bombs. Amidst the chaos, a voice rose above the noise—a voice so beautiful it silenced everyone. It was Cher, standing on stage, singing. The crowd, the police, and even the Hipgnosis henchmen froze, mesmerized. Shannon joined in as a background vocalist, while Adam and Jeremy shut off the fire hose and added their voices to the harmony. The audience stood in awe.

As the song ended, applause erupted into a standing ovation—police included. The henchmen slithered away, drenched and defeated, their equipment useless. It was a crazy finish to the night. Three finalists were selected to continue in the competition: Adam Levine, Jeremy Buck, and, despite her absence, Flor. The judges unanimously agreed along with Andrea and the songwriters and the other musicians that Flor should be a finalist.

The next day, Jeremy Buck and his team hit the road, heading to Port Hueneme for the final leg of the competition. Driving along the Pacific Coast Highway, they approached Malibu. Just before reaching Malibu Colony, they came upon a bridge crossing Malibu Creek. Flash, behind the wheel of Jeremy's rig, started onto the bridge when a semi barreled out of nowhere, sideswiping them. It was Adam Levine's truck, aggressively attempting to force Flash off the bridge.

Flash heard the screech of metal as his truck scraped against the guardrail. Reacting quickly, he jerked the wheel to the right, pushing back against the other rig. Both trucks accelerated, grinding together in a dangerous game of chicken. Then, Flash saw him—a boy standing in the middle of the bridge, staring in disbelief as the two trucks hurtled toward him.

There was no time to stop. With Jeremy's truck pinned against the rail and Adam's rig pressing in, Flash yanked the steering wheel hard to the left, gaining a few inches of space. He veered back to the right, causing the trucks to momentarily bounce apart. With precision, he surged forward, getting in front of Adam's semi. Flash then slammed the wheel left and simultaneously engaged the trailer brakes, keeping his foot firmly on the gas.

The impact was violent as the trailers locked together for a brief moment. Flash's maneuver caused his trailer to swing back, slamming into Adam's truck and knocking it off balance. The other truck veered across the oncoming lane, plowing through the guardrail and plunging into the creek below.

Flash brought Jeremy's semi to a screeching halt and jumped out, searching frantically for the boy. He wasn't under the truck. Flash ran to the railing and scanned the water, but there was no sign of him. Perhaps the boy had managed to jump the rail? Peering into the current, Flash saw nothing.

Jeremy, Joel, and Christopher climbed out of the trailer, shaken but unharmed. Their cargo was scattered across the floor, but their questions quickly turned to the wreckage. On the other side of the bridge, Adam's truck lay on its side, being carried by the current toward deeper waters. Adams crew were swimming, people from shore helping as Jeremy and his team descended to the creek bank, rescuers assisted the last of Adam's team to safety. But Adam was missing. They searched the banks and peered into the water, but there was no trace of him.

Unbeknownst to them, Flor had leaped over the railing just before the trucks collided. The current carried her under the bridge, and by the time she surfaced, she had swum to the opposite shore. Hiding among the rocks, she watched the rescue efforts unfold from a safe distance. Drenched but unscathed, she made her way back to her makeshift camp. She changed into dry clothes and curled up inside a wooden box she used as a bed.

By the time Myles and Madison arrived, crews were pulling wreckage from the lagoon. There was no one inside the submerged truck. Searchers in inflatable boats combed the area, but darkness forced them to call off the search until morning. Myles arranged accommodations for everyone at the nearby Malibu Beach Inn.

When questioned, Adam's driver explained that the truck's autopilot system had inexplicably engaged. The override features were locked out, leaving him powerless to stop or steer. All he could do was hold on.

At dawn, Flor headed to her usual spot along the creek to wash up. Sitting on a sun-warmed boulder, she watched the searchers combing the opposite shore. She was about to leave when something caught her eye—a black spot bobbing between two large boulders down the shoreline. Curious, she approached.

As she drew closer, she realized it was a man's head, his black hair plastered to his face. He was either unconscious or dead. Waves lapped at his head in rhythm, but when she bent down, she saw he was breathing. Flor tried to pull him onto shore, but he was stuck, tangled in branches and seaweed.

Flor waded into the water, diving under to free him. The branches were lodged under rocks, and despite repeated attempts, they wouldn't budge. With the tide rising, she panicked. Grabbing large branches from the shore, she wedged them under his back and neck to keep his head above water, then sprinted up the steep bank.

She stumbled over rocks and branches, cactus spines tearing at her skin, but she didn't stop. She had to find help.

Meanwhile, Myles and Madison were driving back toward the bridge, followed by Flash and Jeremy in the semi. Behind them, Adam's crew rode in a rented van.

As they approached the bridge, a boy suddenly darted onto the highway, waving his arms frantically. Myles slammed on the brakes, narrowly avoiding him.

Flash had to slam on the brakes to avoid rear-ending Mylee's vehicle. He exclaimed that the person ahead was the boy from the bridge accident. Relieved to see the boy unharmed, though frantic, Flash noticed Flor waving and pointing toward the shoreline while speaking to Myles in Spanish.

When Flash and Jeremy approached, Flor motioned for them to follow as she started descending the embankment. By this time, Adam's crew had also joined them, and they all followed Flor. At the shoreline, near two large boulders, they found Adam trapped, his mouth barely above the waterline.

As they attempted to pull him out, it became clear he was stuck. Madison knelt beside Adam, supporting his head on her legs to keep it above water. The others worked together, freeing Adam from the branches and seaweed. Through teamwork, they finally managed to pull him onto the bank.

Madison immediately called for an ambulance while the group carefully carried Adam up the embankment toward the highway. Determined not to let the "boy" disappear again, Flash approached Flor, placing a hand on her shoulder and gesturing toward her scratched legs, indicating she needed medical attention. That's when Flash suddenly realized it wasn't a boy—it was a woman.

They were still gathered around Adam when the ambulance arrived. Adam was conscious as they loaded him onto the stretcher. Before they slid him into the ambulance, he looked at Jeremy and quipped, "You can't drown me, Buck. I'm like a catfish," prompting everyone to laugh.

Another truck pulled up alongside them. When Flor realized who was inside, her expression turned to disbelief. Tears welled in her eyes—it was her mariachi band and her mother.

Myles and Madison could hardly believe their luck. They had found both Adam and Flor Amargo. Adam was going to be fine after a physical evaluation, and now they could focus on uncovering who had sabotaged Adam's truck and blocked Flor's mariachi band and her mother at the border. They also needed to prevent any further attempts to disrupt their plans.

When the group—including Myles, Madison, Jeremy and his group, Adam's team, and Flor's entourage—arrived at Port Hueneme, they were greeted by Andrea, Lumina, and the Europeans.

The bands had already arrived after flying into Los Angeles (LAX) and catching a connector flight to Oxnard. The Port Hueneme annual Banana Festival was in full swing with vendors, education booths, culture booths, and delicious banana-inspired drinks, including banana beer and banana food like chocolate-covered bananas, banana sundaes, and banana cream pie. There were also harbor boat rides, land tours of the port, an antique car show, an amusement area, and of course, music.

The Port of Hueneme's harbor has a depth of 40 feet and accepts vessels up to 800 feet in length. The average rise and fall of tides is 5.4 to 6.0 feet. There are several wharfs, with the Navy having a license agreement with three of them. There's a squid fishery, 600 feet of floating docks, short-haul and long-haul rail connecting to Union Pacific, off-dock port-owned industrial property with Navy and private leases, refrigeration storage, five mobile shore cranes, tugboats, piloting services, stevedores, labor unions, tractor-tide fuel, and security. It handles automobiles, fresh fruit, and is the #1 banana port on the West Coast, as well as breakbulk cargo, general cargo, fish, liquid bulk, and niche cargo.

The seven finalists were ready to start the final leg of the contest, competing for the golden sculpture of Cleopatra, the Temptress Academy's award for best performer. The crowd had ballooned to thousands, and as Bora and Riblja Corba took the stage, about to start playing, there was a huge ruckus in the crowd. It was the Hipgnosis Henchmen Regiment again, marching through the crowd with their horns and drums blaring, interrupting the concert. As they marched towards the stage, there was another huge sound off to one side. It was the sound of bagpipes, percussion drums, and hooves—it was the Alma College Tartan Kiltie Marching Band, Adam Levine's alma mater, with Adam up front, who had been released from the hospital and was one step ahead of the henchmen. They were drowning out the henchmen, much to the delight of the crowd. The henchmen, realizing the tables had turned, soon dropped their equipment and scurried for the exits. As Adam, dressed in a kilt, marched past, Jeremy said to him, "Catfish don't wear skirts," to which Adam replied, "This is my scutes (Catfish armor); otherwise, I'd be naked." Adam grinned. "Catfish don't have scales, their bodies are often naked."

Riblja Corba finished their set to the delight of the crowd, who were now stoked and thoroughly enjoying themselves. Next was Zaz, then Flor, Drazen, and Crvana Jabuka, Sarah, Adam from Maroon 5, who got a standing ovation, and finally, Jeremy Buck and the band. As they started to play, Jeremy was looking out at the skyline and saw a jet in the distance. The aircraft looked like it was tracking directly toward them and was flying very low. Something didn't look right, and after several seconds, Jeremy realized what it was—the jet was flying upside down. It was heading straight toward the crowd. As the jet closed the distance, the roar of the engines grew louder. Jeremy stopped playing, and the crowd's attention turned toward the jet. Jeremy could now see the pilots, their anguished expressions clear on their faces. Just when it seemed unavoidable that the jet would crash into the crowd, a white cloud began to form in front of the upside-down jet.

A memorial Sundial of Alaska air flight 261

It was Cher and the supercomputer. As the nose of the jet entered the cloud, it started to dissipate until the cloud engulfed the jet entirely. The crowd turned back to the stage as Jeremy finished the performance, unaware that the jet had not been part of the act. They erupted in cheers, delighted by the spectacle.

As the competition at the Banana Festival was happening, Andrea and the songwriters had gone out in search of the final two keys. One of the keys was to find a special, near-extinct plant called the soft-leaved Indian paintbrush. This endangered plant was thought to be found only on Santa Rosa Island, but there was a faint occurrence on Anacapa Island, known only by the Chumash through folklore passed down by their elders. It was said this particular occurrence had magical properties, with its pouch-like flowers having bright yellow and black petals. The soft-leaved Indian paintbrush is hemiparasitic, meaning it only grows where a Menzies golden bush serves as its host. Andrea, Lumina, and some Chumash guides would head to Anacapa Island by boat. The blooming flower symbolizes growth, beauty, and the cyclical nature of life, with its vibrant colors and intricate design signifying renewal and new beginnings. It embodies concepts of parity, grace, and the transient nature of existence. It would be the sixth key.

The name Anacapa is a corruption of the Chumash words Eneepah and Anyapax, meaning deception or mirage—a poetic name for an island that shifts its shape depending on the direction of approach. Flocks of seagulls dance around the cliffs, finding crevasses to rest their wings. As Andrea, Lumina, and the Chumash guides approached east Anacapa, the fog thickened, and gusts of wind howled around the cliffs. From the pier, they took the 150 steps up to the tabletop plateau of Anacapa. The Chumash guides led Andrea and Lumina to an eastern point of the island. Looking down from the top of the cliffs, they saw a rocky jetty below where a pod of sea lions rested. A nearly invisible small ledge descended the cliff from where they stood. It led down a few meters to a small patch of earth, hidden from view. This is where they would find the rare, magical soft-leaved Indian paintbrush.

As Andrea and Lumina worked their way down the narrow ledge, the wind ripped at their clothing and threatened to blow them off the cliff onto the jagged rocks below, constantly smashed by the crashing waves. After several minutes of clinging to the side of the cliff and inching their way down, they stepped onto the flat patch of ground, gaining firm footing and catching their breath. At the back of the small indent was a Menzies golden bush, and beside it, the soft-leaved Indian paintbrush, its bright yellow and contrasting black petals looked magical and astoundingly beautiful—perhaps the most beautiful Andrea or Lumina had ever seen. Andrea gently picked one of the smallest blooms and tucked it away in her leather pouch. As they began their climb back up the narrow ledge, seagulls nesting in the nearby crevasses hovered in the gusting winds. First one, then two, then more seagulls swooped at the invaders on the cliffside, and soon, hundreds of them were diving at Andrea and Lumina. They needed their hands to grip the rock face and couldn't swipe at the birds for fear of falling off the cliff. As they clung to the cliff, the seagulls' bombardment prevented them from continuing their climb. The screeching birds clawed and pecked at their faces and clothing. Andrea thought this might be it—that she was about to plunge to her death on the rocks below, eaten by the sea lions—but then the Chumash began to chant.

"Narrow brushstrokes, wide brushstrokes. Crushed by burden, underlying current. The magical Indian paintbrush swirls and swirls, black and gold petals, in all their glory."

The seagulls' bombardment slowly began to dissipate, and Andrea and Lumina climbed the rest of the way up the ledge, where the Chumash helped pull them back to the top of the plateau table.

Tom and Angela, along with their Chumash guides, were headed to San Nicolas Island to the Cave of Whales to find the magic stone—the seventh key.

Access to San Nicolas was tightly controlled by the Navy, which uses the island as a platform for radar and other instruments for tracking missile testing operations. The Cave of Whales and the surrounding beaches are used by sea elephants during their pupping and breeding seasons and are off-limits to the 200 Navy personnel who live and work on the island. The cave is not easy to find. No trail or markings lead to it, and its entrance is not easily seen by anyone walking along the sandstone cliffs that rise from the ocean. Because it wasn't breeding season and was considered a sacred site of the Chumash, the Chumash were able to get permission to visit the cave. When they arrived at the Cave of Whales with the small yacht they had rented, they launched their kayaks and headed for the mouth of the cave. Most of the cave floor was covered in seawater and seaweed. The seaweed attracts swarms of kelp flies, and the kelp flies attract thousands of spiders that feed on them. Black widows lurked in every crack of the cave walls and ceilings, with webs dangling from the ceilings and egg sacs stuffed into the crevices.

The sand floor had long been washed out by the waves, and Tom was getting discouraged. How on earth were they supposed to find a small stone here? It was like looking for a needle in a haystack. The cave itself seemed to be alive, with varying lighting and moisture conditions that illuminated the walls and echoed the sounds of crashing surf. At different times of the day, the sun reflected light that danced across the walls and ceiling of the cave, turning it into an amphitheater.

The sounds of mammals from nearby beaches and shorebirds like gulls and cormorants filled the air. But there was another sound, familiar to the Chumash. It was the sound of a Chumash song stone, a rare artifact that had been hollowed out and had beads inside it. When moved, or in this case, when a gust of wind entered the cave, it produced a faint song. The Chumash led Tom to one side of the cavern wall where a small crevice held the magical stone with a cross inside a circle. As Tom reached in through the spider webs and picked up the tiny boulder, the spiders started coming out from the cracks and crevices, spilling from above. Flies seemed to go into a frenzy as well, buzzing and swarming them. They scrambled for the exit, Angela screaming in fear as she brushed the spiders off her.

As they burst out of the cave and into the bright sunlight, the flies withdrew. They quickly bailed the spiders out of the kayaks and made for the yacht. Tom handed the song stone to one of the Chumash, and as they paddled, he shook the small boulder in rhythm with the paddles, and a song emerged: "Da dah Da Dah Dah da." When Tom let Andrea know they had the magic stone, she told him the next step was to take all the keys to the painted cave on Santa Cruz Island. There, the Chumash would make the offerings and in return, they would learn Christina's location and receive the Song of Seven

Languages. They would meet up at Prisoner's Harbor on Santa Cruz Island.

That evening at Port Hueneme, after the performances, the seven finalists, along with Andrea and the songwriters in attendance, would head to the awards banquet at the recreation center hall. Once they arrived and were seated, Cher came out onto the stage and warmly greeted everyone. She thanked the contestants for entering and performing in the competition and thanked Andrea and the songwriters for their contributions. Cher went on to explain why they had held the competition, revealing Christina's kidnapping, the seven keys they needed to obtain, and the Song of Seven Languages. Languages were part of the reason they had been chosen. Cher explained what they needed to do moving forward: go to the painted cave, make the offerings, and perform the Song of Seven Languages. Cher also revealed that all seven finalists would receive a Cleopatra Award, which drew applause from the crowd.

The contestants were appalled by the news of Christina's kidnapping and were all willing to do whatever it took to help free her.

At Prisoner's Harbor, Tom, Angela, Andrea, Lumina, the seven contestants, and their Chumash guides arrived. The other Chumash guides were already there. The harbor got its name because, after Mexico gained its independence from Spain in 1821, the Mexican government established penal colonies in California, which was sparsely populated at the time.

Penal colonies would expand the Mexican government's presence in Alta California, increase the population, and provide a solution for dealing with Mexican prisoners. In 1825, a small group of prisoners was transported north to Alta California to improve the morals of convicts and to help colonize the area. However, the people living in California opposed the idea, so the plan was dropped.

In 1830, the Mexican government tried again. This time, it contracted with Capt. John Christian Holmes, skipper of the American ship Maria Ester, to pick up 80 criminals in Acapulco and deliver them to California. Holmes tried to drop them off in San Diego and San Pedro but was denied both times, so he next tried Santa Barbara. At the time, Don Romualdo Pacheco was the acting comandante of Santa Barbara's Royal Presidio. Holmes requested permission to discharge his cargo, a routine request. However, once Pacheco learned the cargo consisted of 80 criminals, he said he had to inspect the ship to stall for time. After going below deck on the Maria Ester, Pacheco was horrified by what he saw. The prisoners were living in rat-infested filth, were half-starved, and barely clothed.

He told Holmes that under no circumstances could the prisoners be dropped off on the beach at Santa Barbara, even if it meant facing the wrath of Mexican authorities. The Maria Ester remained anchored off the Santa Barbara shore for several weeks. After being turned down three times, Holmes figured he would be equally unwelcome in Monterey or Yerba Buena. This stalemate lasted for many weeks. Eventually, José de la Guerra, Santa Barbara's leading citizen, persuaded Pacheco to allow a few prisoners ashore to work odd jobs. De la Guerra also provided the men with baths, delousing, and new clothes, all at his expense. These acts of kindness reportedly earned de la Guerra the prisoners' everlasting gratitude. As a result, the prisoners eventually became upstanding citizens of the Santa Barbara area. But what to do with the remaining prisoners?

In April 1830, with the approval of California Governor José Echeandía, Holmes transported and discharged 30 convicts to what is today called Prisoner's Harbor on the north side of Santa Cruz Island. This location was perfect for establishing a penal colony. The Canada del Puerto, a seasonal creek, provided freshwater, and the Santa Barbara Mission provided food, supplies, medicine, tools, and livestock. The prisoners were left to survive and build shelter using tools and local trees and brush. All went well until November, when fire destroyed their shelter and all their supplies. Faced with starvation, the men realized they had to try to make it to the mainland. They built a crude raft and set out without sails, oars, or paddles, entirely dependent on the wind and currents. The men didn't realize that ships were rare in the Santa Barbara Channel in the 1830s, especially in the fall and winter, when southeast storms raged along the Southern California coastline. There was little hope that their raft would be spotted or that they would be rescued.

Legend has it that the raft drifted for days, and the water supply they had brought from the island ran out. Things were looking grim. However, it was one of these storms that saved them. A howling gale drove the raft toward the coast. It held together until it hit the churning surf off what is today Carpenteria. The raft broke apart, throwing all the men into the sea. They were a determined bunch and were close...

To shore, they all made it to the beach alive. The exhausted convicts were rounded up and imprisoned for a time in the Santa Barbara presidio guardhouse. Records show some were flogged as punishment for escaping the island. Eventually, all were freed and absorbed into the community. According to historian H.H. Bancroft, their descendants still live in Santa Barbara and Monterey counties. Today, only the name Prisoners Harbor reminds us of the bizarre events of almost 200 years ago.

As Andrea climbed the rungs of the ladder onto the pier, Tom helped her up with a hand and told her some important news. Myles and Madison had captured Merk Mercuiadis while he was lurking around Port Hueneme and were holding him, though they didn't know how long they could do so. Although all the evidence so far pointed to him and the hypnosis song fund, they didn't have enough information to prove anything yet. Andrea told Myles to bring him with them to Santa Cruz Island. They would take him to the Painted Cave as it would show him that they had figured him and his puzzle out.

The Chumash Polynesian Connection

When Myles and Madison arrived at Prisoners Harbor with their yacht, they had also brought kayaks and a Tomol for the Chumash guides. Tomols were plank-built canoes made by the Chumash. They all went down to the beach, and the conversation came up about the Tomols. One of the Chumash explained that in a handbook written by Alfred Kroeber in 1939, it was stated that there was a definite climax in the Southern California area among the Coast and Island Gabrielino and Chumash, whose culture was semi-maritime with seagoing plank canoes.

Although this climax culture was likely further developed locally once it had taken root on the Santa Barbara Islands, its spontaneous origin on the mainland coast and its growth to the point where it could reach the islands are hard to understand based on either a Californian or a Sonoran-Yuman culture basis. Therefore, there is a possibility that its impetus came in part from the northwest coast or from across the Pacific, to both of which regions there are sporadic but fairly specific parallels: harpoons, canoes, round shellfish hooks, psychological cosmogony… but the abundant archaeological evidence shows that this puzzling local climax culture, as a whole, pre-dates any Caucasian contact. Among North American Indians, only the Chumash and later the neighboring Gabrielino built sewn-plank canoes. In the Western Hemisphere, this technology is otherwise known only from the coast of Chile and among Pacific Islanders. The Tomols were able to carry large loads over long distances, which could allow for navigation across the Pacific. The Chumash believe the Polynesians did reach the Channel Islands off the California coast.

Another Chumash guide then brought up another legend: Santa Cruz Island was named for a priest's staff accidentally left on the island during the Portola Expedition of 1769. A Chumash Indian found the cross-tipped stave and returned it to the priest. The Spaniards were so impressed that they called this island of friendly people La Isla de Santa Cruz, the Island of the Sacred Cross.

Santa Cruz Island resembles a miniature California. At over 96 square miles, it is the largest island in California. It contains two rugged mountain ranges, the highest mountain being Mount Diablo, or Devil's Peak, at 2,428 feet. There is a large central valley/fault system with deep canyons that have year-round springs and streams, along with 77 miles of craggy coastline cliffs, giant sea caves, pristine tide pools, and expansive beaches.

When the conversation died down, they sat listening to the sounds of the rocks and surf. A unique feature of Santa Cruz Island was the sound the cobbled rocks made as the surf washed them first onshore and then retreated. The stones rolled back and forth, clinking and clanking like a stone xylophone. The magic it created was beautiful—clickity, clickity, clack clack click. Afterward, they returned to their yachts. With the faint sounds of the rocks and surf and the gentle rocking of the waves, they drifted into their dreams.

In the morning, they all boarded one of the yachts, except the Chumash, who preferred to be in the Tomols. With the kayaks and Tomols in tow, they set out for Cueva Valdez Harbor, leaving Merk Mercuiadis with a Chumash guide to guard him. At Cueva Valdez, they would anchor the yacht. From there, they would take the kayaks and Tomols to the Painted Cave, or Haxinu Nuwestipa, as it was known in Chumash, meaning "Big Painted Cave."

The mouth of the cave was quite large, over 160 feet high and 100 feet wide. As it had been raining the last several days, a waterfall poured over the entrance, looking like something out of a storybook. Colorful rocks, lichens, and algae lined the cave walls, creating a natural multihued fresco. When they were about two-thirds of the way back into the 1,227-foot-long cave, it narrowed, and as they paddled through, they entered a huge, pitch-black chamber, where a dozen or more sea lions started barking and bawling. The group sat in their kayaks and Tomols, speechless. It was surreal, an indescribable feeling. After several minutes, they paddled past the sea lions and further into the cave.

The Chumash guides, who were in the lead, turned on their flashlights to search for the sandy cave floor. From there, they left their kayaks and Tomols and followed the sandy floor until it turned into a cobblestone floor.

They gathered around at this spot: the Chumash, the seven singers—Adam, Jeremy, Flor, Zaz, Sarah, Drazen, and Bora—along with Andrea, Myles, Madison, Tom, Angela, Tyler, and Angela. The Chumash began their chant as they made offerings of the keys they had collected. First, the plectrum, then the molten pahoehoe toe, and then the Chumash chanted the blessings from the Lady of the Letter. They offered the ceramic tablet of the Whisper Song, and the whole group joined in. With the chanting of the Chumash, the sound in the dark cave was remarkable. Even the sea lions in the distance stopped their barking to listen.

A whisper. A whisper. The wind gently flutters the leaves in the trees. A breeze. A breeze sweeps down to the sea...

The Chumash then offered drops of water from the Tremusa caverns, followed by the magical flower of the soft Indian paintbrush and, finally, the Song's Stone (Tushaut Stone). A Chumash started gently shaking the Song's Stone.

As the songstone started, a vision—crazy, unbelievable—unfolded: There was Christina, on a horse engulfed in flames, a firehorse.

The horse was walking along the rim of a crater, and far below, you could see the bright orange glow of lava—it was a live volcano. Christina wore a flowered reef, and flowers flowed down her long blonde hair. She was in a trance, and as the horse's hooves struck the stone path at equal intervals in a four-beat gait, its head moving up and down in rhythm, Christina was singing in an Adnate tempo. The horse walked along the crater rim, and in the background, you could see Polynesians kneeling and worshipping her, bowing down on their knees. The men were dressed in Malo with Kihei, the women in Ki Kepa. They thought Christina was Pele, goddess of fire and volcanoes.

La la la, la la la, Christina sang in rhythm with the horse's hooves.

As the vision started to fade, seven pages of scripts gently floated down and into the outstretched arms of one of the Chumash, the Song of Seven Languages. The cavern fell back into blackness, and the sound of the sea lions returned. They paddled back through the chamber and toward the light from the mouth of the cave. Hale Maumay was a live volcano on the Big Island of Hawaii, home to the goddess Pele. Hawaii was where the Chumash believed the Tomol came from, across the Channel Islands, 2,000 miles away, thousands of years ago. This was where Christina was: on the crater of Hale Maumay.

They got back to the yacht and headed back to Prisoners Harbor. When they reached Prisoners Harbor, Andrea, along with Myles and Madison, confronted Merk Mercuiadis. Although he didn't admit or deny anything, he told Andrea, with an evil smirk on his face, that the Hawaiian people would never let them get close enough to Christina to free her because they believed she was the goddess Pele.

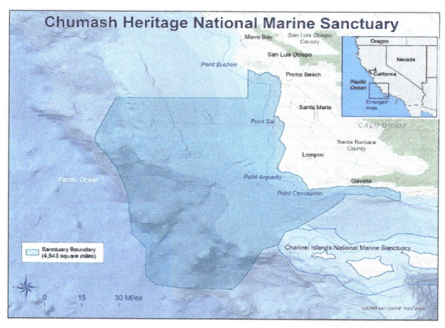

On their journey back to the mainland, they made a little detour to Gull Island, now called Sutil Island, named after a ship from the Galiano Expedition of 1792. The Chumash called it Patsawapr Hooti, which means "House of Cormorants." It is on the south side of Santa Cruz Island, in the transition zone where cold waters from the north meet the warm...

The island is a small rocky outcropping that rises 55 feet out of the water. There are rocky reefs, kelp forests, and submarine canyon habitats for intertidal, nearshore, and offshore species. Colorful sea stars and tiny nudibranchs dot the reef, while California spiny lobsters crowd rocky crevices. Large California sheepshead and kelp bass maneuver through the forests of giant kelp. Purple hydrocoral may also be seen. They anchored here and went for a swim, snorkeling amongst this ocean realm. After the swim, they had lunch up on deck, taking in their surroundings and the view of Santa Cruz Island in the distance. They bid it farewell as they set out for the mainland.

Andrea contacted Cher and updated her on what had transpired at the Painted Cave, mentioning that they had to go to the Big Island of Hawaii, to Halemaʻumaʻu Crater, to free Christina. When Andrea and the songwriters, along with the seven performers and the Chumash guides, arrived at Harbor City, Los Angeles, Cher was there to meet them. She advised that for the time being, they had to let Merck go. Although they had enough evidence against him, it would drag on for months or even years in court, and the Hipnosis song fund, along with Blackstone and BlackRock, would just buy his way out. More importantly, they had to free Christina, and Cher had already made plans to go to the Big Island's Halemaʻumaʻu Crater. As Myles unlocked the cabin and led Merck off the yacht, he was sure he hadn't seen the last of him. Merck insisted he would destroy the Temptress Academy, mumbling about a hostile takeover as he made his way down the dock and disappeared. The next morning, they were heading for Hawaii and Halemaʻumaʻu Crater. The charter yacht Cher had booked, the Agua Azure, was a 60-meter former Royal Navy vessel turned superyacht, which could accommodate up to 30 guests in 15 cabins. Inside, the four-deck Agua Azure featured a brass and ivory interior theme with beechwood and bird's-eye marble furnishings. The salon had a cinema screen, the upper deck a library and a bar with a stylish lounge. The main deck was perfect for al fresco dining. It was also equipped with a plunge pool and a spa. Cher would be aboard and had invited Julie and the main staff. There were also four Chumash guides, the lead members from the lodge: Jeremy, Adam, Flor, Sarah, Zaz, Bora, and Drazen. Then there were Andrea and the songwriters: Tom, Angela, Tyler, Crystal, Myles, and Madison. To entertain the crew and the other guests, the contestants performed, and even Cher gave a set one evening.

On day six, they arrived at Hilo Harbor. They had all rehearsed and mastered the song in seven languages: Jeremy in English, Adam with Scottish roots (hence the kilt), Flor in Spanish, Sarah in german, Zaz in French, Bora in Serbian, and Drazen in Croatian. The song also needed the chant of the Chumash as an underlying element.

They had a long wait for them when they docked in Hilo. It would be roughly a 50-minute drive to Kīlauea Volcano and Halemaʻumaʻu Crater. As they left Hilo on Highway 11 towards Kīlauea and Volcanoes National Park, they drove through Kurtistown and Mountain View. At the Kīlauea Park entrance, they took Crater Rim Drive to the junction of Chain of Craters Road and parked in the

Devastation Trail parking lot. From the parking lot, they would have to walk about a mile on the old Crater Rim Drive road, as it only allowed foot traffic beyond this point. It was a beautiful hike with the pretty koa trees and ʻōhiʻa lehua trees with their vibrant red flowers, mingling with ferns and lichen, and moss covering parts of the lava stones. As they approached the Kīlauea Iki Overlook, there was quite a crowd there: native Hawaiians dressed in traditional attire, men wearing just a malo (loincloth), and women wearing pāʻū skirts with leis made from flowers around their necks. Some were kneeling in worship, leaning forward with their arms outstretched. Others were playing the pahu and pūniu drums, chanting "Aloha ʻĀina" (Love of the Land). There were offerings of food—red fish, bananas, ʻōhiʻa lehua blossoms, and red ohelo berries—piled in front of them, offerings to Pele, the goddess of fire. The park rangers were having trouble controlling the crowd, as some had gone past the roped-off area, and some of the rangers themselves were joining in the chants and worship. Farther down, closer to the rim edge, was Christina on the fire horse, glowing as brightly as the orange lava spewing from vents on the crater floor. Merck was right about one thing—there was no way the Hawaiians would let them just take Christina. Another large crowd of bystanders was milling about, watching the Hawaiians. After a few moments of pause, Cher, Andrea, and the songwriters came up with an idea. They sent the Chumash along with the seven singers down in front of the Hawaiians, so they were between Christina and the Hawaiians.

The Chumash began their chant. The Hawaiians, surprised and shocked, stopped in silence as the seven singers started singing the song of seven languages.

The ruse seemed to be working—until, back in the crowd that had been watching the Hawaiians, a horn began to blow, then another and another. It was the Hipnosis henchmen regiment again, with Merck and his men, and they were drowning out the Chumash and the seven singers with horns, drums, and percussion. The Hawaiians, totally puzzled, stopped chanting and playing their drums, and the scene turned chaotic as the Hipnosis henchmen's full marching band marched toward the Hawaiians, trying to drown out the singers and chants. It was a crazy mix of horns, drums, chants, and singing, and Christina, still in her trance, was singing to the beat of the horse's hooves, echoing off the crater walls.

A lava stream suddenly burst from the crater floor and shot up into the sky above everyone on the crater rim. On top of the glowing orange lava stream was Cher. She started singing as she stood atop the tow of lava. Everyone else fell silent as they listened to her beautiful voice in awe, her melody reverberating through the crowd, her words sinking into the very being of each and every one. Then the Chumash began their chant, and the seven singers joined in with the song of seven languages. It was so beautiful that the henchmen were stricken and frozen. The Hawaiians, too, listened in silence.

When the song finished, Christina broke free from her trance and looked in bewilderment at her surroundings: the Hawaiians, the henchmen regiment, Andrea and the songwriters, the Chumash, and the seven singers. The lava flow was retreating, and Cher stepped off the lava flow as it dropped back to the crater floor.

Myles, who had moved up beside Merck, confronted him and punched him in the face, knocking him to the ground. As Merck fell and hit the ground, some pebbles fell out of his pockets. The Hawaiians, who were watching, became very angry, as taking anything from the crater would invoke Pele's curse. The Hawaiians dragged Merck away, vowing that he would have to put every grain of rock back where he had taken it from and would be severely punished.

As the spell on Christina had been broken, she was now on a regular horse—a very beautiful horse. It had been a wild horse from the Waipi'o herd that roamed the Hawaiian mountain valleys.

When the Hawaiians were explained the events about Christina and Merck's hypnosis, they offered Christina gifts, including the horse and a pā'ū skirt to wear, and invited her to join the parade in the Waimea Paniolo Parade. Cher, Andrea, and the songwriters, along with the Chumash and the seven singers, agreed it would be a fitting end to their journey to join in the festivities beginning in the upcoming weekend.